A Park for the Ages
Beverly's Lynch Park

Historic Beverly

3 Houses, 5 Centuries, 1000s of Stories

Copyright © 2017 by Historic Beverly
All rights reserved. This book or any portion thereof may not be reproduced or used in any manner whatsoever without the express written permission of the publisher except for the use of brief quotations in a book review or scholarly journal.

First Printing: 2017

ISBN 1-891906-15-1

Historic Beverly
117 Cabot Street
Beverly MA 01915

www.historicbeverly.net

Cover image: Frank Marcos

Dedication

This book is dedicated to Virginia Currier, a longtime volunteer for Historic Beverly who deeply loved Beverly history. She was a woman of uncommon devotion who supported many organizations with her time and talent, but Lynch Park was particularly special to her. It was a dream of hers to publish a history of the park, which she began writing prior to her death. We are honored to publish this book in her memory.

Acknowledgments

Ginny Currier's family was very supportive of both her work in researching the history of Lynch Park and of the staff at Historic Beverly as we completed the book. Our thanks go to Bob Currier, Sue Scanlon, Pattie Saltzmann, and Cindy Boccia. Many thanks also go to the following individuals who made significant contributions to this book: Gail Balentine, Edward Brown, Nancy Coffey, Robert Currier, Virginia Currier, Susan Goganian, Pamela Hartford, Frank Marcos, Terri McFadden, Susan Scanlon, Avis Thomas, Tina Torsey, and Martha Wetherill.

Chapter 1
The Early Years: 1636–1775

Woodbury Garrison House
The first frame house built in what was then called "Bass River Side" was a garrison-style house, designed as a place of safety in case of attack by Native Americans. Artist Avis Thomas sketched this house based on other, similar houses from the period. The Woodbury house was torn down in the early 19th century; where it stood is unknown.

17th-Century Settlers

Tradition has it that the first house built in Beverly by an English settler was erected at Woodberry Point, now Lynch Park, in about 1636, by William Woodberry (c. 1587–1676). The house was described as a double garrison and was likely designed for protection in case of attack by natives. Robert Rantoul noted in his journal that the house was demolished about 1807. When Beverly became a town in 1668, much of the land that is now Lynch Park was the property of Captain Thomas Lothrop. Lothrop and his wife

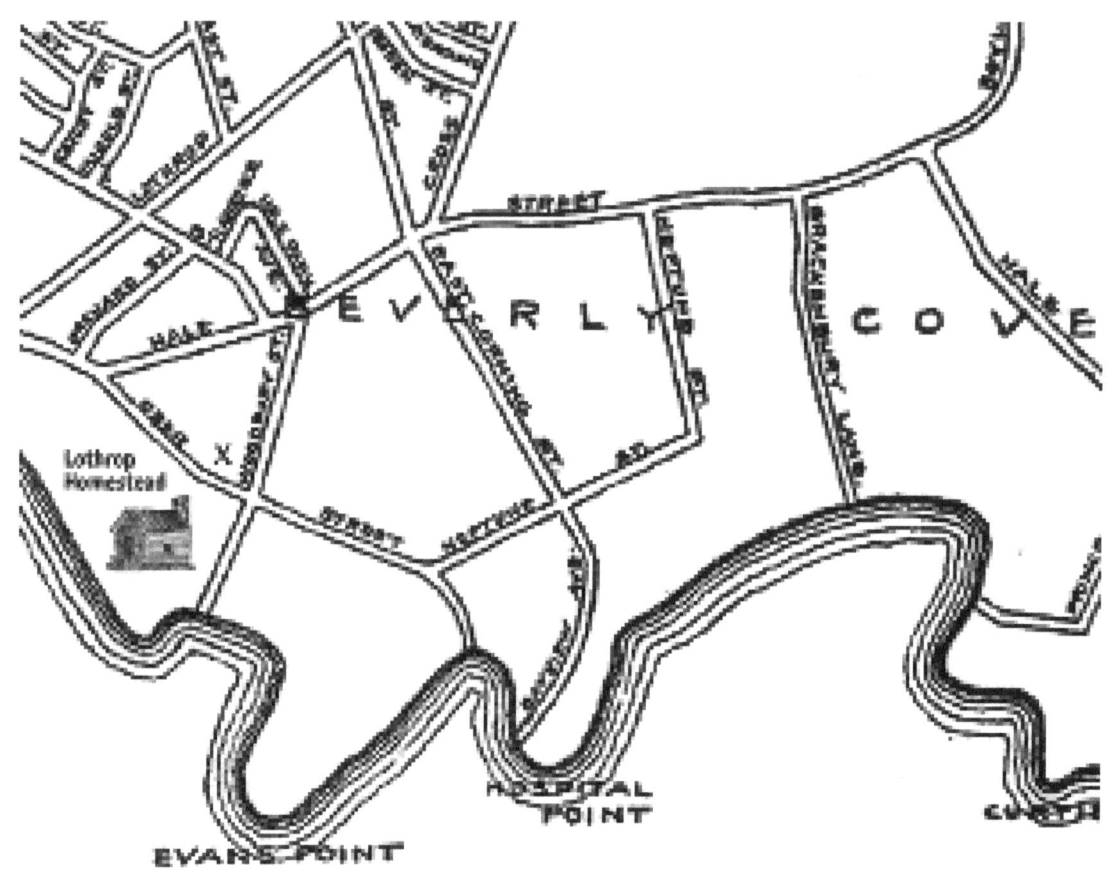

Beverly Cove Map
This map of Beverly Cove shows the original site of the Captain Thomas Lothrop 17th-century house.

Bethia had a homestead of about 10 acres and their house stood on what is now Ober Street, not far from the present park entrance. The captain was involved in the Massachusetts Bay Colony's military affairs almost from the time he arrived in Salem. A veteran of the Pequot War of 1637, Lothrop took an active role as an officer in the militia. Thomas and Bethia were unable to have children of their own, but they took in two young children, Sarah Gott and Noah Fiske. With the outbreak of King Philip's War in 1675, Captain Lothrop was the natural choice, even at age 65, to command the elite company known as the "Flower of Essex" as part of a force of 500 men dispatched by the colony to western Massachusetts to contest the

Islands from Lynch Park
The view of the coastal islands from the shore is one of the few things that have remained unchanged since William Woodbury built the first house here in about 1638.

Indian uprising that was centered there. Tragically, Lothrop's company was ambushed on September 18, 1675, by a vastly superior force of Indians, who slew all but three or four of the soldiers along with 18 Deerfield teamsters who were conveying harvested wheat to military headquarters at Hadley. Unfortunately for the family that the captain left behind, Lothrop went to war without ever writing a formal will. His "verbal will," attested to in court by his widow, was that his house and the ten acres around it would, after

Bethia's death, go to the First Church in Beverly. He also specified generous bequests to Sarah and Noah. His brother-in-law, Boston schoolmaster Ezekiel Cheever, husband of Lothrop's sister Ellen, went to court to claim the estate. He stated that, without a will, Bethia should receive only the minimal widow's portion, and he denigrated the children as "strangers." After four years of fighting him, Bethia, who had remarried, gave up and the estate went to the Cheevers.

In October 1681, Thomas Cheever, acting as attorney for his father, sold the future park property to Thomas Woodberry, grandnephew of the original owner, bringing the property back into the Woodberry family. For nearly 180 years, the area was known as Woodberry's Point.

The Revolutionary Era

When conflict broke out between the American colonies and their British rulers in 1775, Woodberry's Point became a place of defense. On October 10, 1775, the British sloop *Nautilus* chased General George Washington's Beverly-based schooner *Hannah* into Beverly harbor, where the *Hannah*'s crew ran her aground near the present Independence Park. In the resulting action, the *Nautilus* fired a broadside into Beverly, the only time in its history when the town actually came under enemy fire. The conflict between the British and American vessels certainly stirred up and frightened the townspeople. At a town meeting hastily called for October 12, it was voted to take action for defense of the town against any future British incursions from the sea. The town meeting voted to procure four cannon; two nine-pounders and two four-pounders. One of each was to be placed at Paul's Head, known as Hospital Point today. The gun emplacements may still be seen behind the Hospital Point Lighthouse. The other two weapons were to be installed at Woodberry's Point, closer to the main harbor. Additional gun placements were later added at Tuck's Point and the headland west of West Beach.

Work on the embrasures at Woodberry's Point continued through October and into early November 1775. While the breastwork was designed for seven cannon, only two six-pounders were available when work was completed. In July, the Beverly Sea-Coast Company of 45 men, under the command of Captain Moses Brown, had been organized. When members of the company spotted three British ships off Beverly early in December, the town petitioned General Washington for more protection. Breaking precedent by making Beverly the only town in Massachusetts besides Cambridge to enjoy a resident Continental Army force, Washington ordered Colonel John Glover's 14th Continental Regiment to garrison duty in Beverly. By mid-December, Glover's men took up the task of expanding upon and manning the Woodberry's Point fort and Beverly's other coastal defenses until after the British evacuated Boston in March 1776. In August of that year, Glover's Regiment joined Washington, who moved his army to New York, the new theater of the war. The excitement of the war over, the land that would become Lynch Park became quiet once more. It would be another 70 years before the area experienced any significant change.

Chapter 2
The Gold Coast Years: 1846–1936

John Amory Lowell House
Local builder Warren Prince constructed this house on Woodbury Point in 1846 for John Amory Lowell. Robert Evans and his wife, Maria, later purchased it and made it into their summer home, "Dawson Hall." The house was torn down in the 1940s.

The Burgess Homestead at Beverly.

Burgess Homestead
The Lowell house and the beach to the east of it were purchased for $12,000 by Benjamin Franklin Burgess in 1858. Illustration Credit: Lowell/Burgess House from McVey, A. G. "Edward Burgess and his Work." New England Magazine, September 1891. Illustration date unknown. Courtesy of Salem State University Archives and Special Collections.

Summer Residents

During the Gold Coast period, when Beverly played host to many rich and famous summer folk, some important people took up residence on the property that is now Lynch Park. It really started with the railroad. The Eastern Railroad came to Beverly in 1839 and extended north to Newburyport. Then, in 1847, a branch was built from Beverly to Gloucester, opening to Manchester in August and to Gloucester in early December. Wealthy Bostonians began buying up shoreline property. Farmers and mariners laughed up their sleeves at the gullible city men who were paying what seemed to locals to be outrageous prices for rocky land that was useless for farming. In September of 1845, John Amory Lowell, treasurer of Lowell's Boott and Merrimac cotton mills and first trustee of the Lowell Institute, got into the game. He paid Phillip

Walkway to Dawson Hall 1903
Robert and Maria Evans purchased the Burgess Homestead when the property was sold in the late 19th century. The drive and walkway up to Dawson Hall gave a fine view of the house. The granite step leading from the driveway to the walkway can still be seen today just above the building that houses the Beverly Recreation Department.

and Mehitable Hammond $2,400 for 7 5/8 acres on Woodberry's Point, and bought 23 acres on the western half of the point from Cornelius Woodbury, a descendant of one of Beverly's oldest families. Lowell built a house on the end of the point and summered there for 13 years. Warren Prince, a Beverly native who

Mrs. Evans on Her Horse.
Maria A. Evans poses on her horse just outside Dawson Hall in a photo from the early 20th century.

built several homes for the wealthy summer residents, constructed the large house on the point for Lowell during 1846 and 1847. Although long gone, it is still possible to see the front step of the Lowell house.

    In 1858, Benjamin Franklin Burgess, a successful sugar and molasses merchant, paid $12,000 for Lowell's "mansion house and property on Woodbury's Point" as well as for the beach to the east of it. The property's previous name, "Woodberry's Point," was soon changed to "Burgess Point." Benjamin Burgess lost his fortune in the depression of the 1870s and put his Beverly property in his wife's name. When she

Dawson Hall Porch
Wealthy people such as the Evans family came to the coast to escape the summer heat of the cities. The porch at Dawson Hall provided a perfect place to enjoy the sea breeze.

died, Caleb Loring and Augustus Peabody Loring, as trustees of the estate, subdivided it and sold it to William Grover, Albion Turner, and Robert C. Evans.

Grover, a retired Boston merchant, bought the property on Ober Street at the top of the hill in 1882. Turner purchased the property on the east side of the former Burgess home, and built the Queen Anne style "cottage" that later housed President Taft. Wealthy industrialist Evans purchased the Burgess House and five acres surrounding it. A direct descendant of Richard Dawson, Lord of Cremorne, Evans gave his summer home an aristocratic tone when he renamed it "Dawson Hall."

Dawson Hall Parlor
The Victorian-style Dawson Hall was constructed in the mid-19th century by local builder Warren Prince. This interior photograph was taken in the early 20th century when industrialist Robert Evans and his wife Maria summered in the home.

Evans was a self-made man who never went to college. He began his career as a clerk in a Boston rubber company prior to the Civil War. He fought for the Union and earned a commission as captain. He was wounded at the Second Battle of Bull Run, however, rendering him unfit for further service. After the war, Evans married Maria Antoinette Hunt in 1867 and continued in the rubber industry, founding the U.S. Rubber Company (now Uniroyal) in 1873. Leaving that industry to pursue an interest in copper mining,

Grounds of the Evans Estate
The 16 acres that comprise Lynch Park today were for a time three separate summer estates. Robert Evans eventually purchased all of the houses, combining them into a single property. The driveway shown here is still in use. The Carriage House on the right in the photo still stands in the park today.

he became president of the United States Mining Company and was one of the richest men in America when he came to Beverly. A sophisticated art collector, he became a trustee of the Museum of Fine Arts in Boston in 1907.

Over the years that Robert and Maria Antoinette Evans owned the estate, they added several buildings, of which only two have survived to the present: the Carriage House and the former laundry, now used by the Beverly Recreation Department.

Stetson Cottage Postcard
Many postcards were printed showing the summer home of President William H. Taft. Called "Stetson Cottage" after its second owner, theater manager John Stetson, it had 14 rooms. President Taft and his family made this their home during the summers of 1909 and 1910. For the final two years of his presidency, they lived on Corning Street in Beverly.

In 1893 the Evans family acquired a new neighbor, theater manager John Stetson. The *New York Times* reported on October 15 of that year that Stetson had purchased Albion Turner's Queen Anne-style home on Burgess Point in Beverly, next to that of R. C. Evans. Once a circus performer and publisher of racy sporting journals, Stetson made his name after 1868 when he took over management of Boston's Howard Athenaeum, a theater that presented Shakespearean plays and classic opera. He turned it into a vaudeville palace fondly remembered as the Old Howard. A tough businessman, he managed other theaters in Boston and New York, and established Boston's Savoy Hotel. His wife was Kate Stokes, a circus

Evans Estate Carriage House
The Carriage House is one of only two buildings out of several built by Robert and Maria Antoinette Evans that survives to this day. The other remaining building, the former laundry for the Evans estate, is now used as the offices of the Beverly Recreation Department.

performer and accomplished bareback rider. When an injury ended her riding career, she turned to the stage, and, at 26, she married the 51-year-old Stetson in 1887.

    The Stetsons spent only two summers in Beverly. John Stetson died of pneumonia on April 16, 1896, and Kate followed him just three weeks later. They had no children, and when their estate was settled, Robert C. Evans bought the Stetson property, using the 14-room Stetson Cottage as a summer guesthouse until 1909. For the following two summers, President William Howard Taft and his family occupied it.

Taft and Family
President Taft and his family standing near the entrance to the Evans estate, today's Lynch Park. From left, daughter Helen, Taft, wife Nellie, and sons Charlie and Robert.

The Summer White House

In November 1908, Republican William Howard Taft was elected the 27th President of the United States. Not long after he took office, his wife Nellie had a stroke. Although the family owned a summer retreat in Canada, it was thought to be inexpedient for the chief executive to vacation out of the country. Taft sought a summer residence where he and his family could get away from the heat and unhealthy conditions of Washington, D.C., and where Nellie could recover from her stroke. With many of his fellow Republicans

Note from Mrs. Taft
An invitation from Mrs. Nellie Taft to Katharine Peabody Loring to join her at the "Moving Pictures" in Beverly. The Taft family attended social events with many of the North Shore's wealthy residents, including Henry Clay Frick. That particular get-together caused something of a scandal because Frick and Taft were at odds politically.

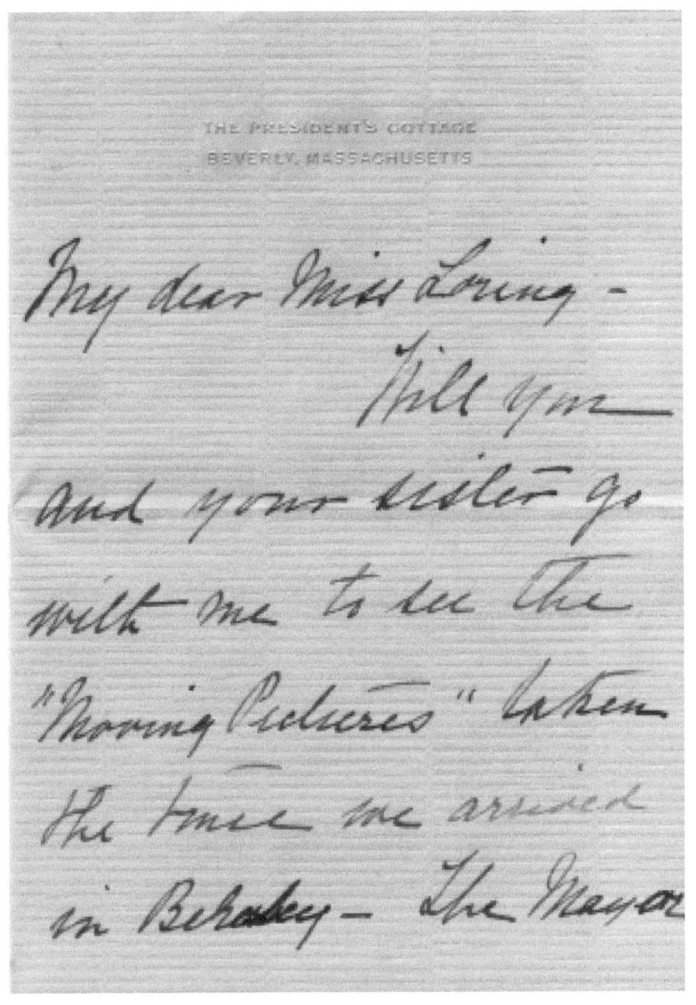

owning or renting homes on Boston's North Shore, this seemed a congenial place to summer. Taft entered into negotiations with Robert and Maria Evans to rent the former Stetson house. Beverly was then able to boast that they were the location of "America's Summer White House."

The Taft family in 1909 included oldest son Robert, age 19, a future United States senator from Ohio, then attending Yale; daughter Helen, 17, a student at Bryn Mawr; and their youngest son, Charlie, a spirited 12-year-old who was fond of getting into usually harmless mischief. The President and his family arrived by train at the Montserrat station on July 4, 1909 and were whisked to the Evans estate. Unfortunately, their arrival coincided with tragedy. Robert Evans had fallen from his horse a day earlier while riding around to inspect his estate, and was hospitalized with what was at first thought to be just a broken rib. The rib had punctured a lung, however, and he died on July 6, leaving his grieving widow to deal with all the commotion surrounding the arrival of her guest, America's president.

Taft thoroughly enjoyed his time in Beverly. His yacht was moored offshore, and he loved playing golf, especially at both the Myopia and Essex County clubs. The President was a great fan of the automobile, and his Sunday drives, accompanied by a Secret Service car, became a local spectacle. President and Mrs. Taft attended worship services at Beverly's First Unitarian Church, and he took part in various civic events, including attending a parade of Civil War veterans and the laying of the cornerstone for Beverly's

Oceanside Entrance to Taft's Summer White House
This postcard shows the oceanside entrance to President William H. Taft's summer home.

new YMCA building on Cabot Street. Taft traveled back and forth between Beverly and Washington as needed during these summers. The once-warm relationship he enjoyed with former President Theodore Roosevelt had cooled when Roosevelt complained that Taft was not carrying out some of the former President's policies. A much-publicized meeting between the two took place in Beverly on June 30, 1910, when they attempted to talk out their differences.

The hoopla surrounding the President, with reporters, Secret Service agents, and tourists swarming about her property, became too much for Maria Antoinette Evans. After the 1910 summer season, she informed Taft that he would not be welcome back to her estate for the summer of 1911. To ensure that

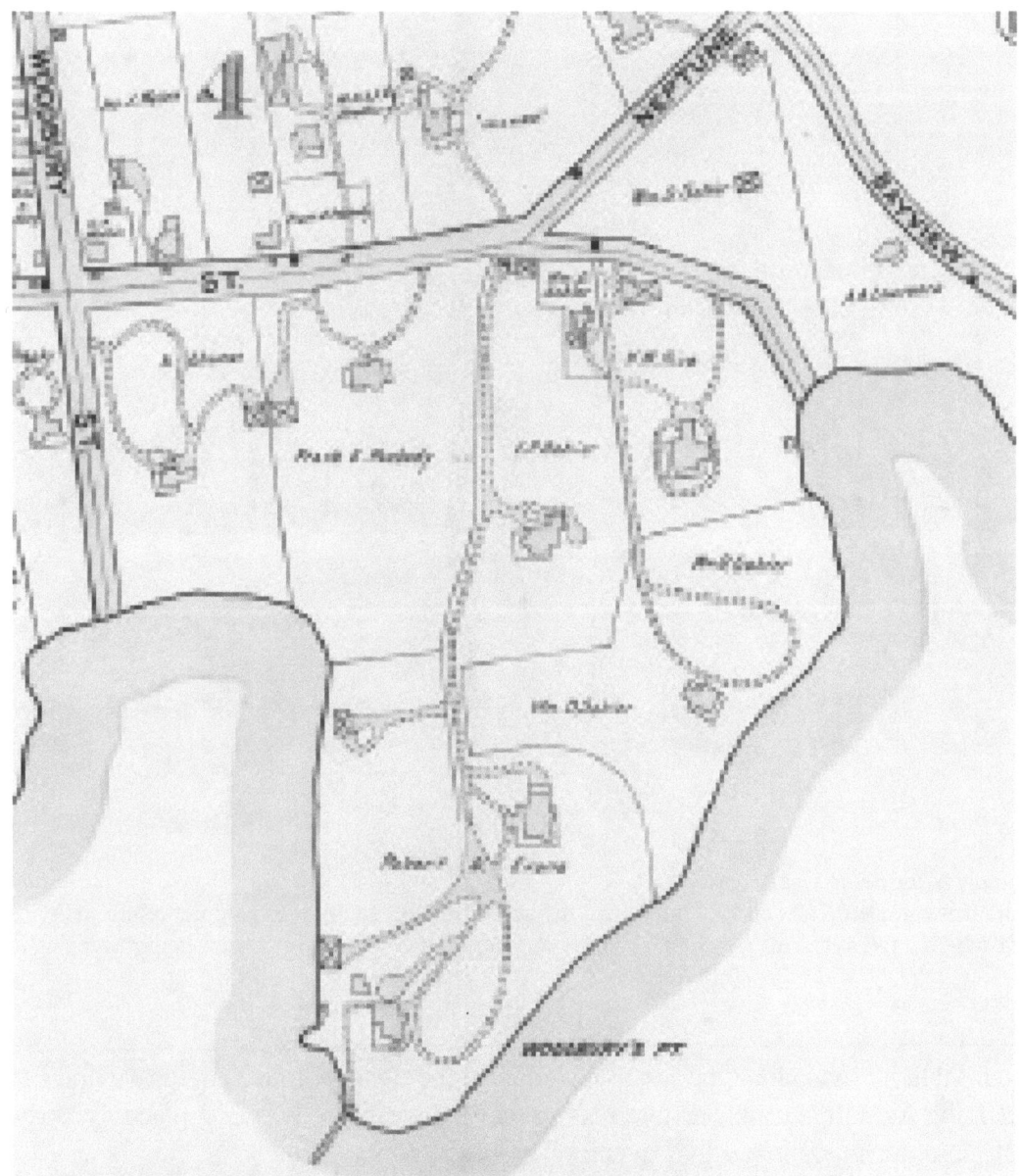

Atlas of Beverly from 1907
This map shows the location of the three large summer homes that once stood at Lynch Park. Dawson Hall was situated on Woodbury Point, Stetson Cottage to the right, and the E. P Sohier home (later called the Monastery) near the driveway from Ober Street.

Stetson Cottage After Being Cut in Two
To make sure that President Taft and his family (and the accompanying commotion) did not return to Stetson Cottage after the 1910 season, Mrs. Evans had the structure cut in two and moved to the beach in preparation for shipping it to Marblehead.

nobody could talk her into changing her mind, she had the Stetson house cut in two and floated by barge to Peaches Point in Marblehead. The famous rose garden was installed in its place. Beverly thus became the only place in the nation to see the "eviction" of a sitting President.

Wanting to stay in Beverly, the Tafts were able to secure summer accommodations for the next two summers at Parramatta, the Corning Street estate owned by the widow of developer Henry W. Peabody. Taft was a one-term president. Theodore Roosevelt, still nursing a grudge, ran in 1912 as a third party candidate, dividing the Republican vote and assuring the election of Democrat Woodrow Wilson. Taft might

Stetson Cottage Floated by Barge to Marblehead
From the beach, the pieces of the house were floated by barge to Peaches Point in Marblehead. Then, on the site where the house once stood in Beverly, Maria Antoinette Evans installed an Italianate garden, part of which still exists today.

not have been overly disappointed in the result, however, as he achieved his lifetime ambition in 1921 when he was appointed to the U.S. Supreme Court.

In 1915, the adjoining estate of Francis W. Peabody was sold to Mrs. Evans. When Mrs. Evans died in 1917, she left all of her Beverly property to her unmarried sisters, Abby and Belle Hunt. Belle Hunt purchased an adjoining house and property from the Elizabeth P. Sohier estate in 1927, completing the outline of today's Lynch Park. The house was built about 1897 by Sohier, but was completely renovated by Miss Hunt. She planned and designed every phase of the rebuilding to make the house a near replica of a villa

Italianate Garden
In 1911, after Maria Antoinette Evans had the Stetson house cut in two and floated by barge to Marblehead, she had an Italian-style garden designed and installed in its place.

that she had occupied for many years in Florence, Italy. The huge front doors were carved with the image of monks who she saw as kind and well loved. For Miss Hunt, this seemed like a fitting image for her new home, which became known as the "Monastery." Many of the decorative elements of the Monastery were imported, including lamps from an Italian cathedral, grille work in the doors, and cork that was used as insulation and then plastered. It took two years to finish the remodeling. For the rest of her life, Belle Hunt summered at her beloved home.

Chapter 3
The Rose Garden

Garden Entrance
The wrought iron gate and decorative scrollwork on top of the brick wall gave a hint of the delights of the walled garden.

Mrs. Evans's decision to remove Stetson Cottage, the Taft summer White House, opened the possibility for a formal garden on the estate. In 1911 the architecture firm of Allen and Collens designed a beautiful Italian-style garden framed by brick walls on three sides, and open to the ocean on the fourth side. Surviving photographs of the garden (many of which appear here) were taken within a few years of completion and show it in its original spectacular state, with the sunken space filled with statuary, covered walkways, fountains, and formal beds of shrubs and flowers.

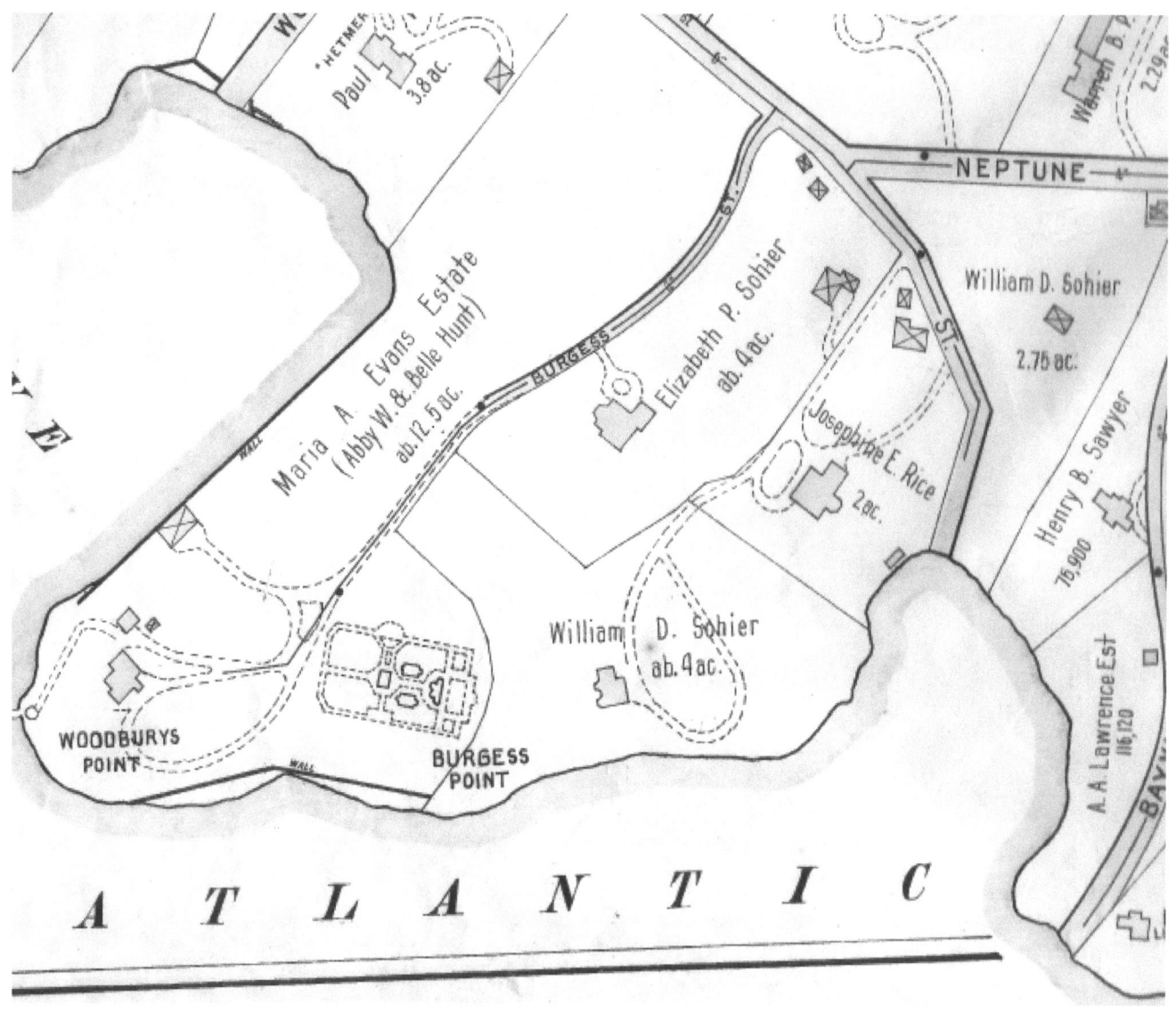

Atlas of Beverly from 1919
A plan of the Rose Garden installed by Maria Antoinette Evans can be seen on the former site of Stetson Cottage.

Rose Garden 1913
Mrs. Maria Evans hired photographers to capture her Italian-style garden on film. This photograph was taken on July 5, 1913, and shows the garden in full bloom.

    Much has survived from the early years of the garden. A columned pavilion on the upper terrace is the site of weddings and countless prom couple photographs. Despite damage from hurricanes and time, the garden still displays a high degree of craftsmanship. The brick wall was built with many forms, shapes, and patterns, including decorative scrollwork made of cast concrete. The marble lions, though somewhat chipped, still retain their charm. The benches are a popular place for visitors to enjoy (continued on p. 26)

Archway and Pillars, 1912
Some of the classical architectural elements and statuary of the early years of the gardens were victims of hurricanes and other disasters, and have not survived. This photograph dates to 1912.

View of the Garden Toward the Ocean
The walled Rose Garden was open on one side to a breathtaking view of the Atlantic Ocean. The marble lions shown on the left of the photo still recline in the garden today.

Garden Structures
These photographs from 1913 show just a few of the sculptures, fountains, and columns that Mrs. Evans and her guests enjoyed. Many of the statues and fountains original to the Rose Garden are gone, victims of time and wear and tear from the elements.

the garden, which today is filled with beautiful flowers and shrubs. The walkways are enjoyed by people of all ages as they stroll through the garden.

The Falconer, a bronze statue on a marble base that is the focal point of the garden, is considered by many today to be a symbol of Lynch Park. Mrs. Evans commissioned this slightly smaller copy of the bronze statue designed in 1872 by George Blackall Simonds (1844–1929). The original statue was set in Central Park and could be seen by the Evans family from their home in New York City. Mrs. Evans had the work erected on her estate in memory of her husband, Robert Evans. The statue depicts an Elizabethan costumed youth striding forward while releasing a falcon from his outstretched left hand.

Although not originally intended as a public space, the Rose Garden is an incredible gift to the city of Beverly. David Lynch, who hoped with his bequest that his hometown would offer parks to be used by local citizens, would certainly appreciate its serene beauty.

Falconer Statue
The bronze statue, *The Falconer,* was commissioned by Mrs. Evans in memory of her husband, Robert. Today, the Falconer is a symbol to many of the beauty of Lynch Park.

Portico and Lily Pond
Positioned on the side of the garden that is opposite to the archway and pillars, stood the portico, flanked by vine-covered arbors and fronted by a lily pond. Although many of these decorative elements have been altered or destroyed over the years, the portico still stands and remains one of the key features of the garden.

Chapter 4
The City Years: 1943–Present

Carriage House
One of two surviving original buildings from the Evans estate, the Carriage House is the site of wedding receptions, parties, and community events. It has been preserved by the hard work of many people who love Lynch Park and are dedicated to its preservation.

Prom Couple
Generations of students from North Shore communities have visited the Rose Garden to have their pictures taken before their high school prom. This photograph was taken in 2008.

North Shore Arthritis Walk
Members of the North Shore Arthritis Walk pose on the lawn in 2011. Many such groups use the park for events and fundraisers.

Camp Program on the Bandstand
Children perform a line dance during one of Beverly's summer camp programs. The bandstand was installed in the 1960s and named for local musician, Alvin Mitchell.

David S. Lynch (1859–1942) was a Beverly native and successful businessman. He and his brothers, Patrick and William, were partners in the Lynch Brothers Leather Company. David Lynch was also vice president of the Beverly Savings Bank, a member of the Knights of Columbus, and a longtime member of the Beverly Hospital Board of Directors. After retiring, David Lynch and his wife, Anne, traveled extensively. Legend has it that on one trip to London, England, the couple visited a park in the center of the city. Mr. Lynch noticed people outside the fence, looking in. Curious, he asked them why they didn't go inside

High Five
People of all ages enjoy the beauty of the park.

the park to better enjoy it. He was told that the park was private and they could not afford the entrance fee. Mr. Lynch was apparently deeply affected by what he heard and decided that Beverly would have a park with free access for the residents of the city. That decision was the first step in the development of what is now known as the David S. Lynch Memorial Park.

In 1936, Miss Belle Hunt willed her oceanfront estate to Beverly Hospital. She thought the location ideal for a convalescent home. The hospital used Dawson Hall for this purpose for about four years, until the property became more of a burden than a benefit.

On June 23, 1943, the city of Beverly purchased the estate from Beverly Hospital for $50,000. The property consisted of 15 acres of land, two houses, Dawson Hall, and the Monastery, a carriage house,

Sledding 1991
Lynch Park is open year round. On snowy days, the park is alive with the joyous sounds of children and adults sledding down the hill that leads to the parking lot. This little boy was having just as much fun being pulled by his father.

laundry building, and an Italianate Garden. This acquisition was made possible through a $400,000 bequest from David Lynch (who had died in December of 1942) for the purchase and maintenance of public parks. The beaches and the grounds of Lynch Park, including the Rose Garden, were available for the public to enjoy by 1945.

Grandmothers and Grandchildren
For many families, the pleasures of Lynch Park are shared. Picnics and the beach, Frisbee and volleyball, kayaking and canoeing are all part of the fun. Lynch Park is truly a park for the ages.

Mr. Lynch's gift was also used for projects such as a bathhouse at Dane Street Beach, and park and playground improvements all over the city. Remaining funds from the bequest were invested and are managed by the David S. Lynch Board of Trustees. These funds continue to pay for improvements to the city parks and playgrounds today.

Of the original properties sold to the city, two buildings still stand. The Carriage House, constructed in the 1890s, is being restored and renovated through the efforts of the Lynch Park Advisory Committee; it is now the site of wedding receptions, parties, art shows, and organizational meetings. The second original building, the laundry house, was converted into offices for the Beverly Recreation Department.

Both large houses that graced the property when the city took ownership are now gone. Dawson Hall was torn down in July of 1943 due to its state of disrepair. The Monastery, used at different times as a tea room run by Charles V. Stromberg, an Art Center for the Guild of Beverly Artists, and a youth center, burned to the ground on June 28, 1966.

Over the years, time and weather have taken their toll at the park. In 1954, major damage occurred from hurricanes Carol and Edna. In 1962, the Rose Garden was nearly destroyed by fire. The Beverly Recreation Department and the Beverly Public Services Department are responsible for the care and maintenance of the park. The David S. Lynch Board of Trustees, the Friends of the Beverly Recreation Department, the Lynch Park Advisory Committee, the Beverly Improvement Society, and the Beverly Garden Club all work to keep the park beautiful. Each year, flowers are planted in the garden, and trees and shrubs are pruned. New trees are added from time to time, adding to the hundreds that provide wonderful shade to visitors. The outstanding job these departments and groups do is on display at every visit to the park.

Whether for sitting in quiet contemplation, searching for shells, swimming, sailing, kayaking, or paddle-boating, its two beaches are prominent features of Lynch Park. The park is designed so that visitors can walk around the entire perimeter, which is bordered by rocks and sparkling water, and take in spectacular ocean views that include Hospital Point Lighthouse, Salem Harbor, Misery Islands, Dane Street Beach, and Independence Park. It is a rare summer day that sailboats are not part of the ocean view.

Italianate Garden Today
Mrs. Evans's garden, known affectionately as the "Rose Garden," has physically changed since its creation in 1911. Yet, despite hurricane damage sustained in the 1950s, fire damage in the 1960s, and an inestimable number of visitors over the decades, the beauty and serenity of the garden has remained the same.

In the shade of graceful trees (some of which are rare species) picnickers, readers, and nappers can pass a hot day cooled by ocean breezes. On the large, open, grassy spaces at the center of the park, children of all ages fly kites, play ball, or attend summer camps. In winter, the huge hill at the entrance to the park provides an ideal slope for sledding.

The city uses the park for events such as the Homecoming Lobster Festival and fireworks. Religious groups hold services there. Music drifts from concerts held at the band shell, built in 1968 and now dedicated to the memory of longtime Beverly resident and musician, Alvin Mitchell.

The Italianate garden is a popular spot for strolling and taking pictures, especially at the weddings that take place there all summer long. Shakespeare's plays have also been performed there. It is a long-held tradition for high school seniors to pose for photos in the pergola before heading to the prom. And, since the late 1990s, people have donated memorial benches along the walkways and ocean's edge, providing visitors a place to sit and enjoy the views.

Rich in history, lovingly preserved, shared from generation to generation—the David S. Lynch Memorial Park is truly a park for the ages.

About Historic Beverly

Historic Beverly has been preserving and caring for Beverly's past since 1891. In addition to housing a collection of nearly a million objects and documents related to Beverly and the North Shore of Massachusetts, Historic Beverly preserves and interprets three historic properties: the Balch House, Hale Farm, and the John Cabot House.

Decorative objects brought back from Asia by Beverly merchants; the papers of William Bartlett, George Washington's naval agent; paintings by artists such as Gilbert Stuart, Frank Benson, Luke Prince, Frederick Coffay Yohn; and more than 400,000 images related to Beverly and the region are among the treasures in Historic Beverly's collections, which are used by scholars, educators, students, genealogists, and residents exploring their neighborhoods.

The Balch House, built in the late 17th century for the Balch family, who were among Beverly's first European settlers, and the 1694 Hale Farm, originally home to John Hale, first minister of Beverly and a key participant in the Salem witch hysteria, evoke New England's roots, early history, and the evolution of Beverly over three centuries. The 1781 John Cabot House, an Essex National Heritage Area Visitor Center, is a museum of Beverly history. Historic Beverly is committed to telling Beverly's stories through lectures, walking tours, exhibits, and publications, and engages the community in a variety of programs.

Historic Beverly is a 501 c3 nonprofit organization funded by the generosity of members and friends. Like many nonprofits, Historic Beverly is fortunate to benefit from the time and talents of many volunteers, without whom we would be unable to serve the public. One volunteer in particular, Ginny Currier, served Historic Beverly and other institutions, for decades, and made this community a better place.

www.ingramcontent.com/pod-product-compliance
Lightning Source LLC
Chambersburg PA
CBHW042019150426
43197CB00002B/79